Exploring the Forest

LEVEL 8
/ou/

Teaching Tips

Purple Level 8
This book focuses on the grapheme /ou/.

Before Reading
- Discuss the title. Ask readers what they think the book will be about. Have them support their answer.
- Discuss the book's focused grapheme: /ou/. Explain that it can have two different sounds: /ow/ or /oo/. Give examples of each, such as *out* and *you*.

Read the Book
- Encourage readers to read independently, either aloud or silently to themselves.
- Prompt readers to break down unfamiliar words into units of sound and string the sounds together to form the words. Then, ask them to look for context clues to see if they can figure out what these words mean. Discuss new vocabulary to confirm meaning.
- Urge readers to point out when the focused phonics grapheme appears in the text. Is it the /ow/ or /oo/ sound?

After Reading
- Ask readers comprehension questions about the book. What kinds of animals and plants were discussed in the book? If you've explored a forest, what did you find?
- Encourage readers to think of words with the /ou/ grapheme. On a separate sheet of paper, have them write the words in two columns: one for the /ow/ sound and the other for the /oo/ sound.

© 2024 Booklife Publishing
This edition is published by arrangement with Booklife Publishing.

North American adaptations © 2024 Jump!
5357 Penn Avenue South
Minneapolis, MN 55419
www.jumplibrary.com

Decodables by Jump! are published by Jump! Library.
All rights reserved. No part of this book may be reproduced in any form without written permission from the publisher.

Library of Congress Cataloging-in-Publication Data is available at www.loc.gov or upon request from the publisher.

ISBN: 979-8-88524-778-8 (hardcover)
ISBN: 979-8-88524-779-5 (paperback)
ISBN: 979-8-88524-780-1 (ebook)

Photo Credits
Images are courtesy of Shutterstock.com. With thanks to Getty Images, Thinkstock Photo and iStockphoto. Cover – Shutterstock. p3 – kpboonjit, Tsekhmister, Hurst Photo. p4–5 – Dajahof, anastasiya adamovich. p6–7 – Dreame Walker, Valsib. p8–9 – manfredstutz, USBFCO. p10–11 – Zmrzlinar, Fauzan Maududdin. p12–13 – nattanan726, RHIMAGE. p14–15 – Gertjan Hooijer, Maryana Serdynska. p16 – Shutterstock.

How many things can you think of that you might find in a forest?

There are lots of different animals and plants that can be found in the forest. Depending on where you are, you will find different animals and different plants growing there.

Take a tour around your local forest.

We should always be careful exploring the forest. Some animals can be dangerous if they are surprised. So, try not to make too many sounds.

Animals might be protecting their young.

Big creatures such as deer, bears, and badgers can be found in different forests around the world. Which big animals can be found in the forest near you?

Never get close to big animals in the wild!

Big animals leave bigger droppings that are easier to find. Fresh animal poop means that the animal is probably still nearby. You can learn a lot from animal poop.

Don't touch!

When exploring the forest, you should try looking up! Lots of forest creatures are tree dwellers. You could find monkeys, rodents, or felines up there.

What could be up there?

Squirrels can be found in most forests because they are tree-dwelling animals. They have bushy tails and eat nuts and seeds.

Squirrels bury nuts to save them for the winter.

A good place to look for animals is near water. Animals go to streams to drink and look for food. Some animals live in, or near, the water.

Don't make any sounds.
You could scare the animals away.

Amphibians are animals that can be found both in and out of the water. These include toads, frogs, and salamanders. Amphibians mostly eat insects and spiders.

What sound does a frog make?

Some forest creatures mostly eat plants, and some mostly eat meat. There is lots to eat in the forest if you mostly eat plants.

The koala can be found in the forests of Australia.

Trees can come in all different sizes. Some are really tall with lots of branches. Some are small and leafy. Trees can also be very old.

Some trees are hundreds of years old!

There are some things that all trees have. All trees have roots that grow underground. They also all have a trunk, which is the main body of the tree.

If you see slime mold on a tree, do not touch it.

If you are going to go up trees, make sure that you have good shoes with good grip. Trees can be fun to play in, but make sure that you are careful.

Say the name of each object below. Is the "ou" in each an /ow/ sound or an /oo/ sound?

house

group

soup

bounce